Joan of Arc

Women of War - Book 2

History Nerds

Joan of Arc
Women of War - Book 2

ISBN: 979-8223258056
Written by History Nerds.

Table of Contents

Introduction

In the annals of history, a select few exist whose lives transcend the boundaries of time and inspire generations to come. Joan of Arc, an extraordinary figure who emerged from tumultuous medieval France, is undeniably one such luminary. In this captivating retelling of her life and deeds, we will embark on an inspirational and enlightening journey, exploring the legacy and the indomitable spirit of this remarkable young woman who defied societal norms and changed the course of history.

Joan lived during the fifteenth century, an era characterized by turmoil and conflict, and the fated duel between two giants - France and England. From that giant war, a single person rose, towering high above it - Joan of Arc. Her story captivates the imagination like no other. Born in the humble village of Domrémy, she hailed from a modest background, seemingly destined for a life of obscurity, but fate had other plans. Joan's profound devotion to her faith, combined with a relentless determination, catapulted her from the fringes of society into the tumultuous world of war, politics, and spiritual fervor.

In this genuinely fascinating account of her life, we aim to shed light on the historical enigma that was Joan of Arc. Drawing upon historical records and the writings of famed contemporary chroniclers, we weave together a tapestry of her extraordinary achievements. So let us delve deep into the annals of war-torn medieval Europe as we bring to life the intricate chaos of politics, religion, and conflict. This chaos formed the backdrop against which Joan's epic tale unfolded. Was she indeed a messenger of God, as she so fervently believed, or an extraordinary individual caught in the throes of a turbulent era?

Chapter I: A Brilliant Vision from God

Joan of Arc, known as Jeanne d'Arc in her native French, was born in the village of Domrémy in northeastern France around 1412 AD. Her parents, Jacques d'Arc and Isabelle Romée, were farmers who lived a simple and modest life. Although details about her early years are scarce, historical records indicate that Joan grew up in a tightly-knit community deeply rooted in the rhythms of rural life. From the get-go, Joan seemed destined for an ordinary life, as befitting to a girl of her station at the time. She had three brothers and a sister and was likely to be married off to a local man of the same social status. As we are about to discover, her life took an extraordinary turn instead. First, however, a little bit about her provenance.

During the early 1400s, literacy was still not widely available to everyone, especially the common village folk. As a result, young Joan was not literate, nor were many of her peers. Because of this, her surname was spelled in a variety of different ways. In contemporary sources, it is written either as "Day," "Tarc," or "Dart." In a letter written by King Charles VII in 1429, she was called "Joan D'Ay." The currently accepted spelling - Joan d'Arc - only appeared 24 years after Joan died. We may never know her surname or if she called herself "Joan of Arc."

Joan displayed many characteristics that set her apart from other girls at a very young age. She was known for her strong will, resilience, and insatiable curiosity that exceeded the boundaries of her village. Despite the limitations imposed upon women in medieval society, Joan yearned to explore the wider world and expand her knowledge beyond the confines of her humble surroundings.

Of course, the events that unfolded in the nation shaped much of her early life. At that time, the Hundred Years' War was shaking the foundations of Europe. It began in 1337, erupting over the English claims to the throne of France and the status of their territories. Most of the conflict occurred in France, which was extremely disruptive to the French economy and people. To make matters worse, France was deeply divided and suffered internal conflicts, mostly centered on leadership. Its King, Charles VI, also known as Charles the Mad, was often unable to rule effectively due to bouts of severe mental illness.

Meanwhile, his brother, Louis the Duke of Orléans, and his cousin John the Fearless, Duke of Burgundy, quarreled bitterly over the regency of France. When John ordered the assassination of Louis, France descended into a civil war. This civil war separated the society into two warring factions, commonly called the "Armagnacs" and "Burgundians." Charles VII, the future King of France, assumed the title of Dauphin (heir to the throne) and was associated with the Armagnac party.

The Armagnacs were a political party or faction led by the supporters of Charles, Duke of Orléans, who was a member of the French royal family. They derived their name from the County of Armagnac, one of the regions where they held significant influence. The Armagnacs were based primarily in southern France and were supported by various noble families, including the powerful House of Armagnac.

On the other hand, the Burgundians were led by the Duke of Burgundy, Philip the Bold, and later by his successors, John the Fearless and Philip the Good. The Burgundian faction was based in the region of Burgundy, which encompassed parts of modern-day France, Belgium, and the Netherlands. They held considerable political and economic power and were known for their wealth and ambitious political maneuvers.

The conflict between the Armagnacs and Burgundians escalated due to a combination of political rivalries, territorial disputes, and conflicting allegiances. The two factions sought to gain control over the French crown and exert influence over the monarchy. The struggle between them led to a series of power shifts and alliances with the English, further complicating the war.

One of the most significant events involving the Armagnacs and Burgundians was the assassination of Louis I, Duke of Orléans, a prominent Armagnac leader and the brother of the French king. Louis was murdered in 1407 by a group of Burgundian partisans, further intensifying the conflict between the two factions. The rivalry between the Armagnacs and Burgundians eventually had a profound impact on the outcome of the Hundred Years' War. The divisions within France weakened the country's ability to resist the English invaders effectively, and the war dragged on for several decades. Of course, these internal divisions in France created a volatile nation whose economy was already troubled by the war with England. Trying to use these divisions to his advantage, English King Henry V invaded France in 1415.

Against this chaotic background, Joan of Arc was born and raised. She grew up, as we mentioned, in the village of Domrémy, which lay at the time in the region called Duchy of Bar. The precise allegiance of this duchy was unclear. It was surrounded by lands that were pro-Burgundian, but most of the duchy's inhabitants were strong adherents of the Armagnac cause, the movement of Dauphin Charles VII. Needless to say, Domrémy was not saved from this bitter war which raged for so long. By 1419, conflicts reached this area of France as well, and in 1425, the village was raided by the English, with many heads of cattle stolen. The poor villagers were bitter, and carried on a widespread sentiment that peace in France would only be achieved when the English were defeated and expelled. During this time, Joan was about thirteen years old.

It was during this time, in her adolescence, that Joan began to experience visions that would later shape her destiny. She claimed to have had divine encounters and heard the voices of saints and angels speaking to her. In 1425, Saint Michael, surrounded by angels, appeared to her in the garden. He was a figure she identified with. Later, she said she wept, wanting these figures to take her with them. Saint Michael appeared to her throughout her life. This saint was seen as the defender of France, and she often saw him - and other visions - when the church bells were rung. To these voices, Joan swore an oath of virginity, and would not marry. These encounters were profound and transformative, leaving an indelible mark on her psyche. Joan believed that these heavenly visitations were a calling from God.

In Joan's early years, a prophecy spread across the French countryside, originating from the visions of Marie Robine of Avignon. It foretold the emergence of a brave young woman who would wield arms to rescue France. Another prophecy, credited to Merlin, also proclaimed that a maiden carrying a banner would end France's anguish. Joan stated that she might be the anticipated maiden, reminding those around her of the belief that a woman would bring destruction to France, but a virgin would redeem it. The authenticity of Joan's visions has been a subject of much debate and speculation throughout history. Some attribute her experiences to psychological or neurological conditions, while others view them as genuine religious phenomena. Regardless, the impact of these visions on Joan's life and the course of history cannot be disputed.

In May 1428, young Joan traveled to the nearby town of Vaucouleurs. There, she petitioned the local garrison commander, one Robert de Baudricourt, to provide her with an armed escort to travel to the Armagnac court at Chinon. The commander scolded her and chased her away. A short time later, in July, the Anglo-Burgundian forces brutally raided her village of Domrémy, for the Burgundian faction had already allied itself with the English, causing further chaos in France. Domrémy burned, its houses destroyed, fields razed, and the folk had to flee in panic. It was an additional reason for the people of this region to stay firmly allied to the Armagnac cause and the Dauphin, Charles VII. In January 1429, Joan returned to Vaucouleurs, again seeking an armed escort to Chinon. Again she was refused, but by this time, she attracted attention. Her claims of visions and her claim to be the virgin that would save France gave her a particular enigmatic reputation. In Vaucouleurs, she received the support of two prominent soldiers, Jean de Metz and Bertrand de Poulengy. Around this time, Joan of Arc received a summons to travel to Nancy directly from Charles II, Duke of Lorraine, who had heard of her. He mistakenly thought she had supernatural powers that could cure his ails.

Joan gave him no cures but scolded him for living with his mistress. Such was her righteous and bold nature.

As Joan's reputation as a visionary spread throughout the region, she faced both skepticism and reverence from those around her. In her own community, some dismissed her as an eccentric or a delusional girl. However, others saw something extraordinary in her eyes - an unwavering determination, a divine spark that could not be easily dismissed. Among those who believed in her was her mother, Isabelle, who saw in Joan a profound sense of purpose and an unyielding spirit. It was because of this that she finally succeeded in her intentions. In February 1429, Joan met for the third time with Baudricourt. This time, he finally agreed to send her to a meeting with the Dauphin Charles VII, after many conversations with Joan and the soldiers who grew to admire her.

At that time, however, the Armagnacs were in a dire situation. The English, allied with the Burgundians, were conquering much of France.

What is more, Burgundians controlled the city of Reims, the traditional site for the coronation of French kings. This dire situation meant that the coronation for Dauphin Charles had not yet occurred, and doing so at Reims would help legitimize his claim to the throne. The worst of all was the pressure on the city of Orléans. By July 1428, it was surrounded and almost entirely isolated from the rest of the territories of the Dauphin. Orléans was a strategically important city, presenting the last barrier on the Loire River before the rest of the Armagnac territories. If the Dauphin lost this town, it would be a bad situation. Later in her life, Joan of Arc testified that it was around this time, with the growingly dire circumstances, that her angelic visions told her she must leave her home at Domrémy, fight for the Dauphin's cause, and help him.

So, Baudricourt finally agreed to send her to a meeting with Charles. Thus, the seeds of Joan's extraordinary journey were sown. Born in a time of immense conflict and political upheaval, she would soon step onto the grand stage of history, clad in armor and driven by an unwavering faith.

Her early life, marked by the simplicity of rural existence and the divine revelations she received, prepared her for the immense challenges and triumphs that lay ahead. In the chapters that follow, we will bear witness to Joan's remarkable transformation from a peasant girl to a renowned military leader. We will explore the intricacies of her interactions with key historical figures, the nuances of the Hundred Years' War, and the profound impact of her unwavering spirit on the course of events.

Chapter II: At the Court of the Armagnacs

Joan of Arc was finally allowed to embark on her fated mission. She was to travel to Chinon, where the Armagnac court, and the Dauphin, resided. Chinon was one of the favorite resorts of French royalty, known for its massive fortress and chateau, lush vineyards, and strategic position. Captain Baudricourt provided Joan with an armed escort of six soldiers and a set of men's clothes. Allowing Joan to wear men's clothes was likely done to make Joan less conspicuous. Nevertheless, Joan continued to wear men's clothes and armor for the rest of her life - she never donned women's clothing again.

The first meeting between Joan of Arc and Dauphin Charles VII occurred in Chinon in February 1429. The voices and visions that Joan kept seeing instructed her to go to the aid of Charles VII, the Dauphin, and help him reclaim his kingdom from the English during the Hundred Years' War.

Meeting the Dauphin, however, was no small

thing. Joan was seventeen years old then, while Charles was roughly ten years her senior. Either way, the audience was granted her at the court, and she explained her mission to the Dauphin. She said that she came to raise the siege of Orléans, and to support Charles and lead him to his coronation at Reims. Joan and Charles had a private exchange, where she left a strong impression on him. It is said that Joan reassured the king-to-be that he was the true heir and a legitimate son of his predecessor, Charles VI.

Before the Dauphin would agree to accept Joan and her mission, he needed more reassurance. He sent Joan to Poitiers, where she had to be examined by a special council of theologians and clerics. They finally decided she was a devout Catholic and a wholly good person. They also claimed that her mission to Orléans could be helpful to the Dauphin. Next, she traveled to Tours, where a team of women examined her closely and confirmed that she was a virgin. With all this, the group of women confirmed that Joan could very well be the prophesied virgin savior of

France, possessing pure religious devotion and purity of soul and flesh.

By then, Dauphin Charles VII was reassured and accepted Joan "into his service." She called herself "Joan the Maiden" and the Dauphin commissioned an extraordinary suit of plate armor, especially for her. Likewise, she was allowed to design her banner and coat of arms and requested that a special sword be brought to her - one that rested beneath the church's altar at Sainte-Catherine-de-Fierbois. In her visions, Saints Michael, Catherine, and Margaret supposedly told her she would find an ancient sword buried there. Thus, she had it brought to her. With all this, Joan the Maiden was ready to embark on her God-given mission. The Armagnacs rejoiced!

Alas, we may never know precisely what happened at Chinon and how the guarded interaction between Joan and the Dauphin went. The private details of their exchange, the way she won Charles over with her zeal and devotion, are things that history does not remember and can only be guessed at. Still, historians agree that the leading motivator of their "cooperation" was Joan's reassurance to the Dauphin that he was the heir to France's crown, having a legitimate birthright and being his father's true son. At that time, many rumors surrounded his birthright - many claimed that the Dauphin was not his father's legitimate son. Allegedly, Joan told him of her vision, in which the Dauphin himself appeared. She said that she knew how Charles, in his desperation, prayed on his knees to God - that if he were not the true heir to France's throne, God should allow him to flee to England, Scotland, or Spain and survive there in peace. Hearing this, the Dauphin was confident that Joan had prophetic abilities as he prayed thus in the privacy of his bedroom. The Dauphin took it as a sign from God, confirming his royal blood and his right to the crown. This confirmation convinced him to renew his battle in the terrible Hundred Years' War.

As we mentioned before, the main point of contention at that time was the city of Orléans. It was an essential strategic hub on the Loire River, and the Armagnacs were besieged there. It was a gateway to the rest of their territories, as the Loire was a dangerous river with only a few suitable crossings. If the English seized Orléans, Dauphin Charles VII would be in a dire situation. Nevertheless, Charles did not see the situation as hopeless yet. The English and the Burgundians began having disagreements about territory. As a result, the Burgundian forces withdrew from the siege of Orléans. The English now questioned whether continuing the operation was in their best interest. Still, the city was besieged and prepared to endure for months. Sieges were the most potent weapon of the Middle Ages - a mighty army needed only to surround a city and starve it into submission. At the same time, they sustained themselves on the surrounding lands. It was simple, it was potent - but it was *slow*.

With the appearance of Joan of Arc, she changed everything. Hearing of the new "prophesied Maiden of France" and her close relationship with the Dauphin, the Armagnac forces found new morale and convictions. Soon, the question of Orléans and the entire Hundred Years' War became a religious conflict. Joan's visions and devotion to God inspired others as well, re-lighting the flames of faith inside them. Before marching out on her military quest, Joan sent a somewhat bold letter to the English commander, Duke of Bedford, in which she claimed that God Himself sent her to drive the English out of France - once and for all.

Ultimately, the Dauphin was convinced about Joan of Arc, that mysterious maiden that appeared "out of the blue" and claimed she was there by God's will to save him and France. Even though he was impressed - he was not entirely free to put significant responsibilities into her hands. That would be simply silly, after all. That is why, in the initial stages of her military career, Joan was still "on the sidelines." Soon, an opportunity arose for her to prove her capabilities and allegiance.

In the last week of April 1429, Joan set out from the city of Blois, a part of a relief army sent to deliver supplies to the besieged forces at Orléans. The city was not 100% cut off, and she entered it on April 29th, meeting with its commander, Jean d'Orléans, Count of Dunois, known as the "Bastard of Orléans". Once within the city, she was greeted by the people and the soldiers with great enthusiasm, as she was seen as an inspiration, a wonder, and a would-be savior of oppressed French people. She rode in on a white horse, adorned in her exquisite armor and brandishing her own banner which was white and adorned with images of saints. To the besieged people, she must have been an amazing sight to behold, and they saw her as a savior sent by God to liberate their city from the English occupation. With Joan's arrival, the morale of the French troops soared. She inspired them with her courage, determination, and unwavering faith. Joan wasted no time and immediately began planning military strategies to break the English siege. However, she was not given formal command or included in military councils.

Nevertheless, she quickly gained the support of the Armagnac troops. She did not shy away from being present where the fighting was most intense, and she frequently stayed with the front ranks. She was not an ordinary maiden, that much was certain to everyone. She gave them a sense that she was fighting for their salvation, and that she was truly on a mission from God. Armagnac commanders would sometimes accept the advice she gave them, such as deciding what position to attack, when to continue an assault, and how to place their artillery. Joan certainly seemed knowledgeable about these things, as she was a quick learner, had a sense of duty and strategy, and made no mistakes. All in all, she took her new military role seriously, and was quick to get a grasp of the army's positions and the enemy's as well.

Under her leadership, the French forces launched several successful attacks on English strongholds, gradually weakening their hold on Orléans. Joan's strategic brilliance and her ability to rally the troops played a crucial role in turning the tide of the war in favor of the French. Joan kept sending the English command letters - urging them to flee France before being destroyed. She'd write these letters and have them tied to crossbow bolts, firing them from the ramparts and into the English lines.

Slowly but surely, the French, bolstered by the appearance of new supplies and Joan of Arc, began driving the English further away from Orléans. On May 4th, 1429, the Armagnac forces of Orléans went on an offensive and attacked a nearby *bastille* called Saint-Loup. Joan was not present during the attack, but once she learned it occurred, she quickly took up her banner, mounted her horse, and rode out hastily to fight. Arriving at the site, one mile east of Orléans, she saw the Armagnac troops retreating in panic, their attack having failed. There she was, her bright banner raised high up, her presence boosting morale and indicating victory by God's will. Joan rallied the retreating troops, re-engaged the attack, and captured the fortress. It was a significant win and a big boost for the Armagnac morale. However, the Armagnac did not yet free Orléans.

There was no fighting the following day because Ascension Thursday was a holy day. Even so,

Joan used the lull in the fighting to send yet another letter to the English, warning them a final time to abandon France. One of these letters, which survives in its entirety, has been addressed directly to the King of England, besides many of his leading nobles. In this letter, Joan speaks of government in religious terms and switches back and forth between the first person "I" and the third person "she" when she refers to herself. Here are the contents of the letter, translated into English:

"JESUS, MARY

King of England, render account to the King of Heaven of your royal blood. Return the keys of all the good cities which you have seized, to the Maid. She is sent by God to reclaim the royal blood, and is fully prepared to make peace, if you will give her satisfaction; that is, you must render justice, and pay back all that you have taken.

King of England, if you do not do these things, I am the commander of the military; and in whatever place I shall find your men in France, I will make them flee the country, whether they wish to or not; and if they will not obey, the Maid will have them all killed. She comes sent by the King of Heaven, body for body, to take you out of France, and the Maid promises and certifies to you that if you do not leave France she and her troops will raise a mighty outcry as has not been heard in France in a thousand years. And believe that the King of Heaven has sent her so much power that you will not be able to harm her or her brave army.

To you, archers, noble companions in arms, and all people who are before Orléans, I say to you in God's name, go home to your own country; if you do not do so, beware of the Maid, and of the damages you will suffer. Do not attempt to remain, for you have no rights in France from God, the King of Heaven, and the Son of the Virgin Mary. It is Charles, the rightful heir, to whom God has given France, who will shortly enter Paris in a grand company. If you do not believe the news written of God and the Maid, then in whatever place we may find you, we will soon see who has the better right, God or you.

*William de la Pole, Count of Suffolk, Sir John Talbot,
and Thomas, Lord Scales, lieutenants of the Duke of
Bedford, who calls himself regent of the King of France
for the King of England, make a response, if you wish
to make peace over the city of Orléans! If you do not do
so, you will always recall the damages which will
attend you.*

*Duke of Bedford, who call yourself regent of France for
the King of England, the Maid asks you not to make
her destroy you. If you do not render her satisfaction,
she and the French will perform the greatest feat ever
done in the name of Christianity.*

*Done on the Tuesday of Holy Week (March 22, 1429).
HEAR THE WORDS OF GOD AND THE MAID."*

The following day, May 6th, the Armagnac forces
resumed their offensive and successfully
captured another fortress, Saint Jean le Blanc,
which the English hastily abandoned. At this
point, the seasoned commanders of the
Armagnac troops wanted to stop their offensive
and rest, but Joan stepped up and urged them to
capitalize on their achievements and continue the

offensive rapidly and launch yet another assault. They eventually agreed to her proposition, and went on to capture the Les Augustins fort, which was built around an important monastery. Joan's incentive proved to be efficient.

The Armagnac command wanted to stop there and was again urged by Joan to press the offensive. The next day they did so, putting even more pressure on the English. They attacked their most important fortress at Les Tourelles. This was the most bitter and ferocious fight yet. At one point in the clash, Joan of Arc stood triumphantly in her trench, raising her monumental banner. Alas, a well-placed arrow struck her at the point between the neck and the shoulder wounding her. She was promptly treated at the rear, her wound proving to be non-fatal. Instead of resting, Joan picked up her banner and returned to the front lines, where she again bolstered the troops' morale and encouraged them to go on one final assault. This proved decisive, and the Armagnacs captured the fortress, driving the English away. The next day, May 8th, the English completely retreated from Orléans, abandoning the siege.

The French forces observed their hurried retreat, but Joan explicitly refused to take further action and pursue them simply because it was Sunday - a holy day. Finally, the English were no longer a threat to Orléans, which was almost surrounded just a few days before. This is a clear testament to the ferocity of the fighting that took place in those several days in May 1429. Of course, it is also a clear insight into the decisiveness with which Joan of Arc approached her new religious and military "career." The city was freed thanks to her - and those fighting by her side.

This major military victory was a cardinal turning point in the Hundred Years' War. After Orléans, one of the most critical Armagnac sites, more English-held fortresses fell within the duchy, causing the English to send more forces to stop the French advance. However, they were quickly defeated, unable to stop the "flood." In just a few weeks, the French swept aside the English from the Loire River Valley, and Bedford, the English Regent of France, lost much of his supplies. This event greatly crippled any English advance for the rest of the year.

Before the events at Orléans transpired, Joan of Arc triumphantly exclaimed to people at Chinon that she was a maiden *"sent by God."* At Poitiers, this claim was questioned by the gathered folk, asking for proof. Joan of Arc replied that she would give them the evidence once she arrived in Orléans. Upon her arrival, Joan of Arc lifted the siege. Thanks to her efforts, many Frenchmen took that as the sign she promised. In turn, the sign furthered her reputation as a genuine religious figure, a prophesied maid that would bring them salvation from the English. Thus, Joan's reputation soared.

Moreover, she received growing support from influential figures and the leading clergymen. The important theologian Jean Gerson and Jacques Gelu, the Archbishop of Embrun, wrote key treaties in her support. The English were not supportive of her. In stark contrast, they dubbed her the "Armagnac whore", a slur that significantly hurt Joan. Reportedly, she bitterly wept when hearing of this epithet. They also claimed that the Devil possessed her, hence her ability to defeat the English armies, even though she was of simple peasant stock. Still, Joan was undeterred and cared little for either praise or insults. She was on a fated mission and would stop at nothing to achieve her quest.

The victory at Orléans was not the end of the war. After this initial success, Joan of Arc left the city and rushed to Tours, where she met with the Dauphin. She implored the leading commanders to quickly advance towards Reims, where they would crown the Dauphin Charles VII, making him King. The Dauphin hesitated at first - the commanders urged him to begin a conquest of Normandy, with which he would possibly turn the tables of the war. Still, Joan's persuasion won the day, and the Dauphin decided that they would go to Reims. Before they did that, the deal stated they would free other occupied towns along the River Loire, namely Beaugency, Jargeau, and Meung-sur-Loire. This cleared the way for the Dauphin and his entourage, who first had to cross the river from Chinon to Reims. The Dauphin also allowed her to join the ranks of her good friend, John II, Duke of Alençon. He and

Joan regularly worked in unison, and the seasoned commander respected her and usually took her advice.

On June 11th, their campaign began. Joan and the Duke of Alençon advanced upon Jargeau, forcing the English to hole themselves within the town walls. Joan sent one of her distinct messages, urging for surrender, but the English refused outright. Due to this, Joan advised a full-on assault upon the fortress. After a day of ferocious combat, the city of Jargeau was taken, and the English forces were defeated. Sadly, the vengeful Armagnac forces killed many of the English that had surrendered or were taken captive. We do not know how Joan reacted to this massacre or how she would've reacted. It was a brutal war, to be sure, and it was 1429, after all. On both sides, there were plenty of reasons for hatred and vengeance, and massacres were not surprising at that time. Joan of Arc, the Maid of God and a staunch Christian, should have reacted with disgust and sadness at such an occurrence. After all, killing captives was thoroughly against Christian principles and the will of God. Then again, even with those principles at play, Joan of Arc took up the sword to smite her enemies, even though the word of God said otherwise.

At Jargeau, Joan was once again at the thick of battle. She excelled in the fight and raised the morale of the troops. A contemporary report tells us that she was amongst the first to scale the siege ladders (a very risky thing to do), holding her bright banner all the while. A stone thrown from the ramparts struck her in the head, splitting her helmet, but not stopping her.

Next, Joan and the Duke of Alençon advanced on the city and fort of Meung-sur-Loire. On June 15th, they captured this vital bridge, and the English holed themselves up in the castle. Instead, the French used this chance to rush towards Beaugency Castle, laying siege to it. After a brief engagement, the English promptly retreated into the castle and were holed up. During this time, Joan met Constable de Richemont, who was highly suspected at the French court. The Dauphin, his advisor Georges de la Tremoilled, and even the Duke of Alençon urged her not to meet him, yet she did. After their meeting, Richemont agreed to help, and the garrison at Beaugency soon surrendered.

In the meantime, the English army from Paris, commanded by Sir John Fastolf, linked up with the troops from Meung-sur-Loire and marched to relieve the siege at Beaugency. The castle's besieged troops were unaware of this and surrendered to Joan of Arc. Realizing what was happening, the English army of John Fastolf retreated toward Paris. They were, however, spotted by the French, and Joan urged the commanders to pursue and devastate them. What ensued was the critical *Battle of Patay*, fought on June 18th, 1429. All eyes were on Joan, who urged for the fight. She calmly exclaimed that she promised a victory more significant than any that Dauphin Charles had won up to that point. Her calm and her confidence inspired the troops once more.

At Patay, the English attempted to replicate the tactics that had brought them victories at Crécy in 1346 and Agincourt in 1415. Their strategy involved deploying a predominantly longbowmen army, positioned behind a barrier of stakes embedded in the ground to impede cavalry attacks. Upon learning about the French approach, Talbot sent a group of archers to ambush them from a wooded area along the road. He then ordered the archers to relocate and establish a concealed position that would block the main road. Thus, they cunningly set-up their long-range archer troops to ambush the Armagnac forces as they advanced. As the English archers hurriedly prepared their new position, they were suddenly attacked by 180 heavy knights from the French vanguard, led by nobles such as La Hire, Xaintrailles, and Hugh Kennedy of Ardstinchar, who was one of the Scottish captains of Joan of Arc's army. The French knights swiftly overwhelmed the archers before they could complete their preparations, thereby exposing the other scattered English units positioned along the road.

Prior to this encounter, the English longbowmen inadvertently revealed their location to French scouts when a lone deer wandered into a nearby field. Unaware of the close proximity of their enemies, the archers raised a hunting cry. Having become aware of the English position, the French vanguard quickly advanced and soon came into view. The French knights successfully neutralized the threat of an ambush, and some were sent back to inform the English men-at-arms about the predicament. Instead of waiting for reinforcements, La Hire, Xaintrailles, Kennedy, and their fellow knights deployed and charged, launching an attack on the exposed flanks of the English positions. Simultaneously, the rest of the French vanguard, comprising around 1,300 men-at-arms, appeared behind the enemy in battle formation after riding over a ridge south of the English lines. Observing the French cavalry charging, Fastolf's unit attempted to join forces with the mounted knights and men-at-arms who constituted the English vanguard. However, the latter fled the battlefield, compelling Fastolf to follow suit. The English forces, outflanked and overrun, faced a protracted engagement with heavy cavalry as the French units pursued the retreating English soldiers, encountering minimal organized resistance.

Historian Juliet Barker asserts that the Battle of Patay represented the most catastrophic defeat for the English since the Battle of Baugé in 1421, and one with far-reaching consequences. The English suffered over 2,000 fatalities out of a total of 5,000 soldiers, and all their senior commanders, except for Fastolf, were captured. According to Grummitt's estimates, English casualties amounted to 2,500, primarily consisting of archers, while the French losses were only around one hundred men. Talbot, Scales, and Sir Thomas Rempston were among the captured English commanders. After his release in 1433, Talbot accused Fastolf of abandoning his comrades in the face of the enemy. Fastolf vehemently refuted the allegation and was eventually exonerated by a special chapter of the Order of the Garter, although his reputation suffered considerable damage.

After a fierce battle, the Armagnac victory was complete - the English were decisively routed. Indeed, Joan fulfilled her promise. The Dauphin received a tremendous and essential victory. On the other hand, the English were suffering one defeat after another. Its reputation of invincibility was quickly dissipating. The near destruction of the English field army in central France, coupled with the capture of several experienced commanders (including the Earl of Suffolk, who was taken prisoner during the fall of Jargeau, and the death of the Earl of Salisbury at the siege of Orléans in November 1428), had catastrophic implications for the English presence in France, from which they would never recover. In the subsequent weeks, the French encountered minimal resistance, allowing them to swiftly reclaim significant portions of land to the south, east, and north of Paris.

Alas, this victory was not capitalized upon. The Armagnac troops should have pursued the defeated English, using the opportunity to boldly strike upon Paris and completely change the course of the war. Instead, however, Joan and the commanders rejoined the Dauphin Charles. At the time, he was stationed at Sully-sur-Loire with his advisor, Tremoille. Upon arriving there, Joan again urged him to rush to Reims and be crowned King. There was a lot of hesitancy, however, as many of his lead counselors advised him to delay, believing the situation was not ideal for the coronation. Joan was fully aware of all the dangers and the situation but feared them not - she was adamant in her reasoning and would not stop her urges. In the end, the Dauphin again agreed to her point of view, urging her counsel above all others. Reims it was!

Chapter III: A Maiden Sent By the Heavens

So, as we see, the war suddenly turned in the favor of the French. A sudden appearance of a miraculous, "God-sent" maiden, a virgin with a penchant for merciless warfare, had raised the Armagnac prospects considerably. She orchestrated the liberation of Orléans, a major city; subsequently, the Armagnac troops decisively broke the English hold on the Loire River and its surroundings. With all this, the "royalist" French army could pursue more significant and critical objectives. However, there were differing views on what the French military should do next. Most of the Dauphin's nobles and advisors urged that he campaign in Normandy, expanding his grasp on France, but Joan of Arc remained adamant that his crowning in Reims was the number one priority. As was always the case, the Dauphin ultimately listened to Joan of Arc.

We ought to remember that this was still the Medieval period, where there existed many *archaic* beliefs. According to tradition, a king-to-be had to be symbolically anointed by none other than God before he can be a true King. Joan was so stubborn about this: she even proclaimed that she would address Charles as "Dauphin," until he officially was proclaimed a King before God. After the Battle of Patay, the French camped at the site for a whole day. The recuperated soldiers ate lunch and finally moved on. Some small intrigues occurred at this time. Count Richemont, a suspicious figure at Charles' court, left a good and honest impression on Joan of Arc, especially after the action at Beaugency Castle. Due to this, Joan urged the Dauphin to pardon Richemont and end the suspicion. Again, the Dauphin listened to Joan, but not entirely. On Joan's request, the Dauphin agreed to end the doubt and "pardon" Count Richemont, but he would not allow the Count to accompany the army to Reims, saying he would rather not be crowned than have the Count present. His word was final, so Richemont took his soldiers and returned to his estates at Parthenay. Ultimately, this was not a favorable solution, as it weakened the Armagnac army. Contemporary accounts tell us that Joan of Arc was greatly displeased by this:

"The Maiden was very displeased, and so were several great lords, commanders, and other counselors."

The remainder of the Armagnac army returned to the liberated city of Orléans. Here, the crowds greeted the soldiers with absolute joy and enthusiasm; everyone was seen as a hero. There were grand celebrations, and the lead nobles and commanders paid their respects at the city's churches. Dauphin Charles was also set to arrive, causing the citizens to decorate the town in his honor. Moreover, men hurried in their dozens to join his ranks and fight against the English. The Dauphin, however, did not arrive, being constantly at odds with his advisors regarding his next move. It was now up to Joan to convince the Royal Council, and the Dauphin, to give the order for the move towards Reims. Convincing them was a difficult thing to do. Before Joan managed to persuade them, as we read above, she had several meetings with Dauphin Charles. One of these happened at St. Benoit-sur-Loire, preserved for posterity through the quill of the Royal French official, Simon Charles. He writes:

Another meeting was held on the 22nd at Chateauneuf-sur-Loire, and the "march on Reims" soon began. By the 24th, the Armagnac army had moved out from Orléans with much pomp. At this moment, Joan of Arc told her close advisor, Duke of Alençon:

From there, it was a 40-mile journey toward the next stop - Gien. From Gien, the formal march towards the coronation point was to begin. This was a city on the edge of Armagnac territories, but even so, the Dauphin arrived before the army and greeted them with much joy as they entered. Now was the time for the future King to formally announce his plans for the coronation - both to his allies and enemies. He wrote customary letters by which he summoned all the leading figures to attend the coronation ceremony. Joan of Arc made letters of her own as well. She was, however, illiterate and had to dictate them. One of these was addressed to the citizens of the city of Tournai in Flanders. This city was deep in Burgundian territory but still free from its control and independence. The reason for this was simple: the town paid a hefty sum to the Duke of Burgundy and thus "stayed out of it." Joan's letter to the town's inhabitants was likely a way to win them over to the cause. In it, she describes their glorious victories and asks the town officials to attend the coronation. The letter survives in its entirety and is an excellent insight into the tone, attitude, and character of Joan of Arc. It was sent on June 25, 1429. The surviving copy in Tournai's archives was preceded by a paragraph that reads:

"And because we know that you always desire to hear good tidings of the condition and well-being of the King our lord, we have caused copies to be made of the letters which the Maiden, who is currently with the

King our lord, has sent to us, consisting of the following..."

"+ Jesus + Mary +

Noble loyal Frenchmen of the town of Tournai, the Maiden informs you of the tidings from here: that in eight days she has driven the English out of all the places they held on the River Loire, by assault and otherwise, where there were many killed and captured; and she has defeated them in battle. And know that the Earl of Suffolk, La Pole, his brother, Lord Talbot, Lord Scales, and my lord John Fastolf and many knights and commanders have been captured and the Earl of Suffolk's brother and Glasdale are dead. Stand fast, loyal Frenchmen, I pray you. And [crossed-out word] I pray and request you to be ready to come to the anointing of the noble king Charles at Rheims, where we will be soon. And come to us when you learn that we are approaching. I commend you to God; may God watch over you and grant you grace so that you can maintain the good cause of the Kingdom of France. Written at Gien, the 25th day of June.

To the loyal Frenchmen of

the town of Tournai."

Still, the march to Reims was not entirely unopposed. The obstacles that the Armagnacs encountered along the way were quickly dealt with. Beforehand, Charles sent messengers to the Burgindian towns of Bonny-sur-Loire, La Charite, and Cosne, saying they ought to obey him. They all refused. In response, Charles sent a small army under Louis de Culan, quickly forcing Bonny-sur-Loire to surrender. While they were still at Gien, the army of Joan of Arc received its meager pay. This fact is a direct insight into two things: that the Armagnacs were not in an ideal situation; and that they valued their leaders more than the pay. In contemporary accounts, the lack of funds did not dissuade the troops, but they were willing to serve nonetheless, many declaring that they were willing to go wherever she (Joan) would go. Such was the presence of Joan of Arc, inspiring and encouraging.

At Gien, Joan and her closest commanders, unable to wait any longer, were very impatient to begin the march and left earlier to set up camp some 12 miles east of the city. At long last, the Dauphin "took the hint" and ordered the march to Reims to begin. The campaign finally started on the feast day of St. Peter, on June 29th, 1429.

Around the time the march began, one interesting event transpired. This anecdote is the ideal glimpse into the type of character Joan of Arc was - deeply religious and devoted to the purity of body and soul. What happened? After the troops moved out of the city, Joan noticed that several of them were distracted by a group of prostitutes that lurked around the army. Their distraction enraged her to no end. She swiftly reacted, punishing the sinful soldiers. She drew out her sword and struck several of them with the flat of the blade. As she did so, the blade snapped in two. Luckily, it was a replacement blade, not the unique relic she retrieved from St. Catherine de Fierbois church. Yet even so, Dauphin Charles mistakenly thought it was that sword and scolded Joan, telling her she should use a baton instead next time. Joan expected purity from soldiers, commoners, and nobles alike. We also see that even though she was a young maiden, she still commanded respect and authority, being at liberty to punish her soldiers. It was that attitude that inspired the troops and ensured their unwavering loyalty.

It was written that once the army was underway, the troops were gallant, bold, brave, and very courageous, even though they were entering a region of France full of fortresses and towns garrisoned by the English and Burgundians. According to contemporary sources, the troops numbered around 12,000 - a solid number. Many of these were, however, lesser landholders with poorly-equipped soldiers. They all flocked to the army, eager to serve under Joan of Arc, the maiden of France.

The Burgundians and the English were now increasingly nervous. After several defeats, they were no longer as confident and cocky as before. Numerous unsettling reports began appearing. On June 1st, the Burgundian commander, Philbert de Moulant, leader of the troops stationed at Nogent-sur-Seine, sent a letter to the Rheims leaders, reporting the Armagnac Royal army sighted nearby. Moulant assured the leaders that Auxerre and all the other towns in the region did not care about "the Armagnacs nor the Maiden." He also promises aid to Rheims if they "had any trouble with her."

Auxerre, in particular, was a dangerous threat to the marching Armagnac army. Because of this, they decided to take a detour to this town, as otherwise, it would threaten their rear. The town leaders of Auxerre defiantly refused to render complete obedience to Charles out of recognition of their allegiance to the Duke of Burgundy, who had been given the town in 1424. The commanders, therefore, made preparations for a siege. Before anything came to fruition, the commanders quickly abandoned their plans for the siege. The reason for this was bribery. Dauphin's advisor, Lord Tremoille, was paid a sum of "two thousand écus" by the citizens of Auxerre so he would call off the siege. Since Tremoille had influence at court, he accepted. These events greatly angered the other Armagnac commanders, Joan included.

Following a three-day break, the host advanced in a northeastern direction covering eighteen miles to reach the town of Saint Florentin, which promptly surrendered. Subsequently, they charted their course towards the city of Troyes, where the treaty that disinherited Charles had been ratified nine years earlier. By July 4th, the army had arrived at St. Phal, conveniently close to Troyes.

Afterward, a series of letters ensued. Joan dispatched a letter to the inhabitants of Troyes, urging them to:

"wholeheartedly pledge their allegiance and acknowledge the rightful authority of the esteemed king of France, who will imminently be present in Reims and Paris, regardless of any opposition he may face. With the assistance of King Jesus, he shall establish his rule in the sacred territories of his kingdom."

Detailed accounts from the opposing side vividly depict the events that unfolded. On the 5th day, the leaders of Troyes composed a letter from their vantage point "upon the walls," surveying the assembled forces against them. They reported that the "enemy in person" had arrived before the city at nine o'clock in the morning. The garrison, comprising approximately 500 English and Burgundian troops, tried to repel the Armagnacs but were eventually pushed back into the city after fierce combat. As the citizens of Troyes adamantly refused to surrender, the besieging army settled in for a prolonged siege. However, the situation soon turned more arduous for the attackers than the defenders: the army faced severe shortages of provisions, resulting in several thousand men lacking essentials like bread. The troops gathered raw beans and wheat directly from the fields to sustain themselves. It is mentioned that the abundance of beans was attributed to the sermons delivered during the preceding winter by a Franciscan friar named Richard. Friar Richard had advised the citizens to "plant extensive quantities of beans" in preparation for "the arrival of a significant figure." While it remains uncertain whether he had the Royal army in mind, the soldiers expressed gratitude for the beans, even though such meager sustenance fell far short of their accustomed provisions.

This raises an interesting question: what were military rations like during the Hundred Years' War? Modern rations, made with chemical preservatives, were nothing like those used in medieval times. Food rations in the middle ages were much more robust and healthier when available. Contemporary figures often complained about nobles and high-ranking mercenaries who insisted on having large portable ovens to eat fresh-baked pies while on a campaign. The common soldier likely had far less than that. The example of eating raw beans is the perfect example. For Joan's army, this meager diet only caused further problems - as hunger gripped the troops, they were inevitably compelled to steal food from neighboring farms, disregarding Joan's explicit prohibition against such acts of plunder. Simon Beaucroix recounted an incident during the campaign, likely at Troyes, wherein a Scottish soldier informed Joan that the piece of meat she had just consumed had been obtained through the theft of a calf, potentially by himself. Beaucroix reports that Joan was so angered by this revelation that she attempted to strike the Scot in her anger. Yet another example of how strict and disciplined Joan of Arc was - not only in religious matters but in all other spheres of life as well.

Troyes proved to be a challenging new event. As the situation grew increasingly uncertain, Dauphin Charles summoned a gathering of his nobles and tasked them with determining whether they should abandon the siege. The majority expressed their support for withdrawing the army. However, an older council member named Robert le Maçon proposed an alternative approach. Recognizing that the enemy knew about their limited resources from the outset of the campaign, and the trust in Joan's guidance initially prompted their endeavor, he suggested seeking her counsel before reaching a final decision would be prudent. Upon consulting with Joan, she conveyed to the group that if Charles opted to remain positioned before the city, they would successfully capture it within a span of two to three days,

Here was another clairvoyant moment from Joan. She then mounted her great warhorse, "a baton in her hand," and skillfully organized the soldiers to bring large bundles of sticks and anything else wooden, doors, tables, window frames. Swiftly and efficiently, the soldiers - under Joan's guidance - began filling the impassable moat, erecting siege works, and setting up their cannons. Reportedly, Joan did all this *as could have been done by a commander who had been nourished all his life in war."*

The following day, as the city leaders of Troyes surveyed the ongoing preparations, they reached a similar realization. With an impending assault on the horizon and Joan herself issuing the command to commence, the city's prominent citizens emerged to propose negotiations. Among those who arrived to meet her was Friar Richard, the same individual credited with the bountiful fields of beans. Joan recounted that he approached her cautiously while sprinkling holy water, which she found amusing. In response, she called out,

"Approach with confidence, for I shall not flee."

Friar Richard was incredibly inspired by Joan of Arc, claiming she was Divinely inspired - i.e., inspired by God. He made her one of several female visionaries with whom he associated himself.

In the end, the Siege of Troyes was a victory. The garrison pulled out, inciting a minor incident. Joan of Arc met them at the gate and refused to allow all their prisoners to be evacuated and continue their captivity. Dauphin Charles agreed to Joan's pleas and paid a small ransom for each captive, thus ensuring their freedom. Around nine o'clock in the morning, the triumphant army entered Troyes. Joan organized rows of archers along the road creating a welcoming display for Charles and his nobles. Thus, with Troyes captured, the Armagnac army had a clear path toward Reims. The Dauphin's coronation was near at hand.

Chapter IV: A Swift Rise and a Swift Downfall

On July 14th, the Armagnac army arrived at Châlons-sur-Marne, and the city swiftly opened its gates in welcome. At this location, Joan of Arc encountered several individuals from her hometown of Domrémy, including Jean Moreau - to whom she gifted one of her garments - along with four other villagers. They were journeying to Reims in response to Charles' invitation to attend the coronation. Although Joan had seen these familiar faces just a few months earlier, the passage of time must have made it feel like years.

It is believed that Châlons-sur-Marne is where Joan's cousin, Nicholas Rommée (de Vouthon), a clergyman from the Cistercian Order, joined her. His monastery was situated in the diocese of Châlons. According to a surviving document, Joan requested his services as a chaplain and almoner in her army. Charles ordered the Abbot of Nicholas' monastery to grant him permission.

On the 15th, the army departed from Châlons and set its course towards Reims. The realization of

Joan's mission was now drawing near. Around twelve miles from the city, at the chateau of Sept Saulx, Charles halted his army, giving rise to fresh concerns. According to an eyewitness, there was apprehension that insufficient artillery would jeopardize the entire campaign. However, Joan reassured him by saying,

"Do not worry. The townspeople of Rheims will come out to welcome you."

Her words proved to be accurate - yet again. The Burgundian commanders of the city's garrison, the Lord of Chatillon-sur-Marne and the Lord of Sauveuses, departed with their troops after informing the citizens that they would return with reinforcements if the city could hold out for a maximum of six weeks. The dust had barely settled from their departure when the citizens decided not to endure a prolonged resistance. Consequently, when the army approached on Saturday, July 16th, the citizens willingly surrendered the keys to the city.

Towards evening, Charles entered the city and was welcomed by the citizens who greeted him with joyous shouts of "Noël!" This traditional greeting, reserved for kings and beloved leaders, had been used since Charlemagne's coronation on Christmas Day, hence the use of "Noël." The enthusiastic pro-Valois sentiments of the citizens surfaced once they realized that Charles liberated them from the presence of armed Burgundian troops.

As control of the city was transferred, many Anglo-Burgundian supporters hastily departed, including Pierre Cauchon. For Cauchon, this would become a recurring pattern as Joan's army continued its advance from one city to another. He would harbor lasting resentment towards Joan for the defeats that shattered his faction's aspirations of imminent victory, ultimately forcing him to flee from his home region and diocese. His memories of those events would neither fade nor prompt forgiveness toward her.

Again, letters were sent inviting key figures for the upcoming coronation. Being now at Reims,

Joan of Arc dictated yet another important letter. It was addressed to Duke Philip of Burgundy, and sent on July 17, 1429, reminding the duke of a previous letter asking him to attend the coronation.

Burgundy was one of the six secular Peers of the kingdom expected to attend such a function, along with a matching set of six ecclesiastic Peers. Still, the Duke was allied with the English at the time and therefore supported Henry VI as king of France. In this second letter, she asks the Duke to "make a good firm lasting peace" with Charles.

"+ Jesus Mary +
[in a later hand: "17 July 1429, at Rheims"]
Great and formidable Prince, Duke of Burgundy, Joan the Maiden requests of you, in the name of the King of Heaven, my rightful and sovereign Lord, that the King of France and yourself should make a good firm lasting peace. Fully pardon each other willingly, as faithful Christians should do; and if it should please you to make war, then go against the Saracens. Prince of Burgundy, I pray, beg, and request as humbly as I can that you wage war no longer in the holy kingdom of

France, and order your people who are in any towns and fortresses of the holy kingdom to withdraw promptly and without delay. And as for the noble King of France, he is ready to make peace with you, saving his honor; if you're not opposed.

And I tell you, in the name of the King of Heaven, my rightful and sovereign Lord, for your well-being and your honor and [which I affirm] upon your lives, that you will never win a battle against the loyal French, and that all those who have been waging war in the holy kingdom of France have been fighting against King Jesus, King of Heaven and of all the world, my rightful and sovereign Lord. And I beg and request of you with clasped hands to not fight any battles nor wage war against us - neither yourself, your troops nor subjects; and know beyond a doubt that despite whatever number [duplicated phrase] of soldiers you bring against us they will never win. And there will be tremendous heartbreak from the great clash and from the blood that will be spilled of those who come against us.

And it has been three weeks since I had written to you and sent proper letters via a herald [saying] that you should be at the anointing of the King, which this day, Sunday, the seventeenth day of this current month of

Differing perspectives emerged regarding the shifting tides of war. News of the forthcoming coronation attracted fresh troops to Joan's army, commanded by notable figures such as the Lord of Commercy and Lord René d'Anjou. The latter individual held considerable significance, much like many influential figures of the time, as his political and familial circumstances were intricately intertwined. His lands, claims, and relatives were scattered across central Europe. Initially, due to pressure from his uncle, the Duke of Bar, and his father-in-law, the Duke of Lorraine, he had been compelled to pledge loyalty to the English in exchange for his duchy of Anjou in northwestern France. However, he would soon reject that agreement and align himself with his brother-in-law, Charles VII. As both a Duke and a claimant to the Kingdom of Sicily, Lord René d'Anjou insisted on leading the Royal army. Notably, he was only twenty-one years old.

Another significant duo of personal importance to Joan of Arc arrived during this period. Within the financial records of Rheims, a brief entry indicates that "the father of the Maiden" (and according to another source, her mother as well) lodged at an inn named "L'Ane Rayé" ("The Striped Donkey"), situated opposite the cathedral. The town covered their accommodation expenses during the coronation. It is remarkable how even the tiniest fragments of information can capture the most poignant moments in history. For our heroine, the most poignant of moments was quickly approaching. On July 17th, Joan's proclaimed mission reached its climax. The majestic Reims cathedral, adorned with the banners of prominent Armagnac faction nobles and filled with a crowd eagerly anticipating the coronation, served as the magnificent backdrop for this momentous occasion. The Dauphin Charles was to become King Charles VII.

For this occasion, in a solemn procession, the revered vial containing the anointing oil, known as "la saincte ampoule" in medieval French, was ceremoniously escorted on horseback by four appointed commanders: Lords Saint-Sévère, Culan, Rais, and Graville. They accompanied Abbot Jean Canard as he reverently carried the precious relic into the cathedral. This sacred oil was instrumental in the coronation. Furthermore, according to tradition, the coronation necessitated the presence of twelve specific secular and ecclesiastical dignitaries. However, due to the division of France amid the warring factions, adjustments had to be made. The Duke of Alençon assumed the role that would have belonged to the Duke of Burgundy while a clergyman filled in for Cauchon. To compensate for the absence of three other lords, Guy XIV de Laval (the young man mentioned in a previous letter) was elevated to the rank of Count and joined the Counts of Vendôme and Clermont as representatives. The ceremony extended from nine o'clock in the morning until two o'clock in the afternoon. During the proceedings, Charles received a knighthood from the Duke of Alençon, and the Archbishop of Rheims placed the crown upon his head. Lord Pierre de Beauvau, an eyewitness, described in a letter to the Queen that the joyful exclamation of "Noel!" echoed throughout as trumpets resounded, causing the church's arches to tremble. Throughout the ceremony, the Maiden steadfastly stood by the King's side, holding her banner. After the King was crowned, a touching scene unfolded before all the gathered folk. Joan of Arc, devoted to her lord and king, knelt piously on both her knees and embraced the king's legs. She "wept hot tears" and said:

"Noble King, now is accomplished the will of God, who wished me to lift the siege of Orléans, and to bring you to this city of Reims to receive your holy anointing, to show that you are the true king, and the one to whom the Kingdom of France should belong."

Contemporary sources state that many of the gathered figures wept along with Joan.

So it was that Joan's original mission was fulfilled. Following her visions, she achieved an immense task and crowned Charles VII King of France. It was, indeed, as if God sent her. Still, her mission was not yet complete. The King was crowned, true - but the war was not over. The time came for another campaign.

Chapter V: The King and the Heretic

With Charles now crowned King, the tables in France were turned in favor of the Armagnac party. Following the crowning, the royal court engaged in negotiations with the Duke of Burgundy, resulting in a fifteen-day truce. During this period, the Duke of Burgundy pledged his efforts to facilitate the handover of Paris to the Armagnacs while also pursuing ongoing discussions for lasting peace. After concluding the treaty, Charles led his army on a comprehensive expedition through the Ile-de-France region, where he received the allegiance of each city one by one. In the vicinity of Crepy-en-Valois, Joan expressed her desire for God's permission to return to her family's residence. However, when the truce ended, the Duke of Burgundy broke his promise and failed to fulfill his commitment. Because of this situation, Paris became the next target for the Armagnacs. While Joan and the Duke of Alençon advocated for a swift advance towards Paris, disagreements within Charles's court and ongoing peace talks with Burgundy hindered the progress, resulting in a slow march. As the Armagnac army neared Paris, numerous towns along their route surrendered without resistance. However, on August 15th, the English forces led by the Duke of Bedford opposed the Armagnacs near Montépilloy, occupying a fortified position that the Armagnac commanders deemed too formidable to launch an assault against. Trying to provoke the English into attacking, Joan of Arc boldly rode out in front of their positions, tempting them.

Alas, the English stood firm and did nothing. The result of this was a standoff. On the following day, however, the English retreated. Afterward, the Armagnacs were free to continue their march on Paris. They reached it by September 8th and were quick to assault it. A staunch Burgundian supporter, Governor Jean de Villiers de L'Isle-Adam, defended the city. Now, even though the Burgundians had just 3,000 soldiers within the city walls, they also had the support of all the city's inhabitants. The latter thought the Armagnacs were intent on razing the city to the ground and thus decided to defend it at all costs.

What ensued was a vicious blood bath. King Charles VII ordered the assault - Paris would be taken by storm. He gave the honor of leading the attack to none other than Joan of Arc, his maiden heroine. Joan and her army bravely charged the city's gate, trying to cross the water-filled defensive moat. Casualties were numerous, with Armagnac soldiers falling dead left and right, showered by missiles from the city walls. The attackers could not progress and failed to capture the gatehouse. In the process, Joan was wounded in the thigh by a crossbow bolt. She was barely evacuated from the battlefield and taken behind the lines to recuperate. Even in her wounded state, she wished to continue the attack, disregarding the mass casualties. King Charles said otherwise and ordered a full retreat of the Armagnac troops, seeing that no progress was made. After this brutal and short battle, the citizens of Paris successfully defended their city - with minimal losses.

Suddenly, Joan's role began dwindling. Paris was an unnecessary and foolish defeat, and the Royal court of King Charles no longer saw her in the same light as before. The loss reduced their faith in her. Moreover, her fierce independence and constant advocacy for battle and marching began to conflict with the Royal court's desire to find a diplomatic solution with the Burgundians. Just like that, she was no longer that bright and illustrious maiden that turned the tide of war. She fulfilled her mission, crowned the king, and with the first defeat she experienced, the court cast her aside. Scholars at the University of Paris even argued that she failed to take Paris because her inspiration was not divine. Had her divine guidance run out?

Paris was the fated crossroad in Joan's story.

On the 13th, the troops commenced their arduous journey back to the Loire. By September 21st, the army had returned to Gien and was disbanded. Perceval de Cagny, the squire and chronicler of the Duke of Alençon, summarized this event concisely and resentfully: "Thus, the determination of the Maiden and the King's army was shattered." Like many others who had served in that army, Cagny believed that the disastrous policies advocated by the Royal counselors, with

Georges de la Tremoille being singled out for blame, had fatally undermined Joan's achievements. This was the secret to the shadowing of Joan. The King was ill-advised, and the nobles of his inner circle ran his policies. It was no secret that many of them held views different from Joan's. The commanders were dispersed to their estates or former areas of operations. When the Duke of Alençon, preparing a campaign into Normandy, asked that Joan of Arc be allowed to join him, but the Royal court refused.

After the army was diminished, Joan was relegated to the background. She was moved around several Royal estates until a suitable task was found. Such a task appeared in October. Joan was given the command of a moderate force and tasked with defeating Perrinet Gressart, a notorious mercenary in league with the English and the Burgundians. The man was with his troop at the town of Saint Pierre le Moutier, and the forces under Joan laid siege to it. An intriguing anecdote survives from this attack. After a brief siege, Joan ordered a full-on attack, as before. Jean d'Aulon, Joan's squire and protector, recollected that the initial attack had ended in failure, with the soldiers retreating, except for Joan and a small group of men standing by her side. He approached her and advised her to withdraw alongside the remaining troops, but she adamantly refused, asserting that she had "fifty-thousand" soldiers by her side. Urging the army to bring bundles for filling the town's moat, she launched a fresh assault that astonishingly seized the objective "with little opposition," as described by the amazed d'Aulon. The city thus fell on November 4th.

The next target in this small campaign was the town of La-Charite-sur-Loire. However, it is worth noting that the Royal Court did not support Joan's army in this campaign. Running low on supplies, Joan of Arc was left to fend for herself. Thus, she wrote several letters to nearby towns, asking for their help. Here is one of them:

"Let it be remembered that the Maiden Joan, messenger of God, and my lord of Albret, sent a letter to the town of Clermont on the 7th day of November

The attack on La Charite was, sadly, an utter disaster. Joan was in a difficult situation from the start: the November weather was freezing, she had few men at her disposal, supplies were low, and there was no support. According to her bodyguard, Cagny, the King *"made no diligence to send her food supplies nor money to maintain her army."* After a month of preparations and a siege, Joan of Arc abandoned the mission. In her hurried retreat, she was forced to leave her artillery - a costly move. Because of this, her reputation dwindled even more, and she lost more favor at the court. She spent the rest of the winter at various Royal estates while the English and Burgundians regrouped for a new campaign. Upon return to court, however, she discovered that King Charles was honoring her and her family. She would be made a noble so the King could show his gratitude for her service.

Throughout December of that year, she was dormant, with her service not needed. During the Easter period (April 22nd), Joan found herself in Melun, where she later recounted that her saints had foretold her capture "prior to Saint John's Day" (June 24). She had expressed on numerous occasions that being captured and betrayed were her greatest fears.

In the meantime, the Burgundian army remained in motion despite assurances of peace. Then, on May 6th, Charles VII and his advisors finally acknowledged that the Duke had manipulated the Royal Court. In a letter that day, Charles conveyed that the Duke had "diverted and deceived us through truces and other means."

He ordered a series of detrimental offensives on Burgundian territory towards the east. However, the Armagnacs encountered difficulties in the northeastern region as the Duke of Burgundy had amassed a significant presence there. Employing a strategic plan outlined in a comprehensive document, the Duke aimed to seize the bridge at Choisy-au-Bac, followed by the monastery at Verberie. Subsequently, an organized sequence of attacks would be carried out to cut off all supply routes leading to Compiègne, which had refused to surrender according to the terms agreed upon the previous year.

On May 16, Choisy-au-Bac fell into their hands, and on the 22nd, the Duke commenced a siege on Compiègne. Witnessing the bravery displayed by the city in its defiance, Joan could not allow it to succumb without aid. Reinforced by an additional 300-400 troops gathered at Crepy-en-Valois, at sunrise on the 23rd, she and her small army covertly entered Compiègne. Some historians suggest that Joan's expedition to Compiègne was a desperate and treasonable action without the court's or the King's documented permission. Others, however, have argued that she could not have launched the expedition without the financial support of the court. The actual circumstances of this action remain unknown to us.

Perhaps it was fated, and in her visions she knew that she *must* be present in the city. Joan possessed foreknowledge of the impending events. As per the later testimonies of two individuals who, as young boys, had been part of a gathering of curious children observing Joan as she prayed in a church in Compiègne that morning, it was apparent that she was deeply distressed in her soul. She confided in the children, urging them to *"pray for me, for I have been betrayed."* Later that day, Joan was at the head of a small force that led a foray out of the city, attacking an enemy camp at Margny. However, during the attack, the party was ambushed by a cunningly hidden Burgundian force, which lay in wait behind a hill called Mont de Clairoix. Now effectively trapped outside the city and pinned against a river with no escape, Joan was surrounded by enemy troops. When asked to surrender, she refused outright, still sitting atop her war horse. She was, however, ignored and quickly pulled down to the ground by an enemy archer. A Burgundian nobleman, Lionel de Wandomme, made her his prisoner. A contemporary chronicler writes that the Armagnac troops were devastated by the capture of their heroine, Joan of Arc. On the other hand, the Burgundians and the English, having captured their bitter enemy - rejoiced. The chronicler writes:

"[The English and the Burgundians] were overjoyed, more so than if they had taken 500 combatants, for they had never feared or dreaded any other commander... as much as they had always feared this maiden up until that day."

The commander of the garrison in Compiègne, Guillaume de Flavy, immediately fell under suspicion as a potential traitor, although concrete evidence of his guilt was never established. Given that the Royal Court was divided into factions at the time, each vying to eliminate prominent leaders supported by their rivals, it is plausible that a small group within the Court may have betrayed Joan. However, the available evidence suggests that Charles VII was likely not among the guilty parties, contrary to common claims. Records from the Morosini, who was in contact with the Royal Court, indicate that Charles VII attempted to compel the Burgundians to release Joan in exchange for the customary ransom. He also threatened to treat Burgundian prisoners per the treatment Joan received. The University of Paris, which was pro-Anglo-Burgundian and later played a role in orchestrating her conviction, sent a concerned letter to John of Luxembourg, reporting that the Armagnacs were exerting considerable effort to secure her return. Dunois and La Hire led four military campaigns during the subsequent winter and spring, apparently aimed at rescuing her by force.

Unfortunately, these rescue attempts proved unsuccessful, and the Burgundians refused to negotiate a ransom for her release. Upon capture,

Joan was quickly moved to the castle at Beaulieu-les-Fontaines near Noyes. Here she quickly made her first attempt to escape but failed. She was transferred to Beaurevoir Castle as a result. She made another escape attempt, jumping from a tower's window and landing in a dry moat. Alas, she was injured but survived. In November, she was finally moved to the Burgundian town of Arras, where escape was impossible.

At this time, the English and the Burgundians negotiated for the "purchase" of Joan of Arc. These negotiations were successful - the English paid 10,000 livres to the Burgundians to have Joan transferred to their custody. They promptly moved her to the city of Rouen, the leading English headquarters in France. Once she was in English hands, King Charles VII seemingly failed to save or free her. Joan was now in the hands of her bitter enemies- the English - who passionately hated her. They would go to any lengths to have her tried and condemned - and removed as an opponent. The job of procuring Joan and setting up a trial was given over to the prelate and Bishop of Beauvais, Pierre Cauchon, a strong advocate of the English in France and a staunch Anglo-Burgundian supporter. In simplest terms, Cauchon was tasked to "orchestrate a murder" in the guise of an Inquisitorial religious trial. Moreover, many of those involved in the trial were paid hefty sums and "rewarded" even before the trial began. Numerous surviving documents record in stunning detail the payments made for these reasons. Furthermore, later testimonies confirmed that the trial was mainly conducted for revenge against Joan rather than a genuine trial for expected accusations.

Chapter VI: A Tragedy of Epic Proportions

Once in Rouen, Joan's tragic fate begins to form. She was shown no respect or understanding by the English and was troubled at every step. Despite the inquisitorial procedure stipulating that suspects should be held in prison under the supervision of the Church, with female prisoners guarded by nuns to ensure their safety, Joan was instead confined in a secular military prison where English soldiers served as her guards. According to multiple first-hand testimonies, she expressed grievances about the soldiers' repeated attempts to rape her. In response to this threat, she clung tightly to her soldiers' attire and secured her hosen, hip boots, and tunic with numerous cords. This was her sole method of protecting herself against potential rape, as traditional dresses did not offer such a defense. Regrettably, the tribunal later exploited this situation by accusing her of violating the prohibition on cross-dressing, deliberately disregarding the exemption granted in cases of necessity by medieval doctrinal sources like the "Summa Theologica" and "Scivias." Witnesses recounted that Joan implored Cauchon to transfer her to a Church prison where she could be guarded by women, enabling her to wear a dress safely. However, her request was never granted.

In prison, she was interrogated. One of the interrogations was penned down and survived in its entirety. Here it is:

"Will you refer yourself to the judgment of the Church on earth for all you have said or done, be it good or bad? Especially will you refer to the Church the cases, crimes, and offenses which are imputed to you and everything which touches on this Trial?"

"On all that I am asked I will refer to the Church Militant, provided they do not command anything impossible. And I hold as a thing impossible to declare that my actions and my words and all that I have answered on the subject of my visions and revelations I have not done and said by the order of God: this, I will not declare for anything in the world. And that which God had made me do, had commanded or shall command, I will not fail to do for any man alive. It would be impossible for me to revoke it. And in case

the Church should wish me to do anything contrary to the command which has been given me of God, I will not consent to it, whatever it may be."

"If the Church Militant tells you that your revelations are illusions, or diabolical things, will you defer to the Church?"

"I will defer to God, Whose Commandment I always do. I know well that that which is contained in my Case has come to me by the Commandment of God; what I affirm in the Case is, that I have acted by the order of God: it is impossible for me to say otherwise. In case the Church should prescribe the contrary, I should not refer to any one in the world, but to God alone, Whose Commandment I always follow."

"Do you not then believe you are subject to the Church of God which is on earth, that is to say to our Lord the Pope, to the Cardinals, the Archbishops, Bishops, and other prelates of the Church?"

"Yes, I believe myself to be subject to them; but God must be served first."

"Have you then command from your Voices not to submit yourself to the Church Militant, which is on earth, nor to its decision ?"

"I answer nothing from my own head; what I answer is by command of my Voices; they do not order me to disobey the Church, but God must be served first."

"At the Castle of Beaurevoir, at Arras or elsewhere, had you any files?"

"If any were found upon me, I have nothing to say."

Several hearings were conducted from February 21st to the end of March - 1431. Typically, Inquisitorial tribunals followed the practice of gathering witness testimonies against the accused and rendering a verdict based on such evidence. However, in this case, the only witness summoned was the accused herself. As a result, the trial assessors, as some later confessed, resorted to attempting to manipulate her into making statements that could be used against her. These actions represented significant departures from proper legal procedures, indicating further irregularities in the trial. Joan was accused of heresy, blasphemed by wearing men's clothes, acting upon "demonic" visions, and refusing to submit to the Church, claiming that she could be judged "by God alone." Many of these accusations are petty and only half-true, especially about "cross-dressing." Even the authority of the trial tribunal was questionable. Standard procedures required those who tried an accused person to be unbiased or non-partisan. In this case, it was the complete opposite. Normally, that would render the trial *null and void*, but not in this case. Furthermore, the accused person had the right to appeal to the Pope. It is reported that Joan of Arc repeatedly asked that the court honor these rules but was ignored each time.

Early in the trial, the tribunal attempted to accuse Joan of witchcraft, claiming that her banner was "endowed with magical powers" and that she "poured wax on the heads of small children." Later, these charges were dropped and were not included in the final list of accusations. Initially, an incredible 70 articles of accusation were prepared. The 70 were ultimately reduced to 12.

During the trial, Joan of Arc was incredibly calm and composed. She showed great control over her actions, and the witnesses were impressed by her composure and prudence when answering questions. In one instance, Joan was asked if she knew she was *in God's grace*. This was a trick question and was meant as a scholarly trap. Church doctrine held that nobody could be certain of *being in God's grace*. If she answered "yes," she would have been charged with heresy; if she said "no," she would have confessed her guilt. With great prudence, Joan avoided the trap by saying, *"If she was not in God's grace, she hoped God would put her there, and if she was in God's grace, then she hoped she would remain so."* Contemporary accounts state that those present were stunned and impressed by her answer.

Seeing that they could not force Joan to submit willingly, the court stooped so low as to present to her the instruments used for torture, hoping to scare her into submission. Joan did not even flinch, and was not moved by the sight of the cruel devices. Even so, the court voted whether

Joan should be tortured, but the majority of the votes were against.

On May 23, Joan received an official admonishment from the court. The following day, she was taken to the churchyard of the abbey of Saint-Ouen for public condemnation. As Cauchon began reading Joan's sentence, she consented to submit. She was presented with a document of abjuration, which included an agreement stipulating that she would refrain from bearing arms or wearing men's clothing. The contents of the document were read aloud to her, and she affixed her signature to it. At the time, public heresy was a capital crime in which an unrepentant or *relapsed heretic* could be given over to the judgment of the secular courts and punished by death. Having signed the abjuration, Joan was no longer an unrepentant heretic. Still, she could be executed if convicted of relapsing into heresy. This was the groundwork of the trap that Cauchon hoped to lay for Joan of Arc.

The final step of laying that trap was related to the heretical cross-dressing charge. Several witnesses testified later as to what happened. Joan of Arc ultimately consented to wear a dress after signing the abjuration. She was, however, shaved bald and kept in chains. Almost at once, attempts to rape her increased to an unbearable frequency. The guards constantly harassed her and were joined in by a "great English lord" who also wanted to rape her. To force her into the trap, the guards stripped her of her dress and threw her only the old male clothing. She was *forbidden to wear it,* however. Ultimately, facing hypothermia, Joan of Arc was forced to dress in the male clothes she was left with. Promptly, Pierre Cauchon pronounced her a "relapsed heretic," condemning her to death.

Several eyewitnesses remembered that Cauchon came out of the prison and happily exclaimed to the Earl of Warwick and other English commanders that were waiting outside: *"Farewell, be of good cheer, it is done!"*, implying that he had orchestrated the trap that the guards had set for her, and that Joan of Arc was to be murdered.

So it was that at about the age of nineteen, Joan of Arc was executed on the 30th of May, 1431. In the morning hours before the execution, the maiden was allowed to receive the sacraments, despite the court process requiring they be denied to heretics. Afterward, she was taken to the Old Marketplace in Rouen (Vieux-Marche), where her sentence of condemnation was publicly read. Here it is in its entirety:

In the Name of the Lord, Amen.

"At all times when the poisoned virus of heresy attaches itself with persistence to a member of the Church and transforms him into a member of Satan, extreme care should be taken to watch that the horrible contagion of this pernicious leprosy do not gain other parts of the mystic Body of Christ. The decisions of the holy Fathers have willed that hardened heretics should be separated from the midst of the Just, so that to the great peril of others this homicidal viper should not be warmed in the bosom of pious Mother Church. It is for this that We, Pierre, by the Divine Mercy, Bishop of Beauvais, and We, Brother Jean Lemaitre, Deputy of the renowned Doctor, Jean Graverend, Inquisitor of

the Evil of Heresy, specially delegated by him for this Process, both Judges competent in this Trial, already, by a just judgment, have declared this woman fallen into divers errors and divers crimes of schism, idolatry, invocation of demons and many others.

But because the Church closes not her bosom to the child who returns to her, we did think that, with a pure spirit and a faith unfeigned, you has put far from thee thy errors and thy crimes, considering that on a certain day you did renounce them and did publicly swear, vow, and promise never to return to thy errors and heresies, to resist all temptations, and to remain faithfully attached to the unity of the Catholic Church and the communion of the Roman Pontiff, as is proved at greater length in a writing signed by your own hand. But after this abjuration of your errors, the Author of Schism and Heresy had arisen in your heart, which he had once more seduced, and it had become manifest by thy spontaneous confessions and assertions - O, shame! -that, as the dog returns again to his vomit, so have you returned to your errors and crimes; and it had been proved to us in a most certain manner that you have renounced thy guilty inventions and thy errors only in a lying manner, not in a sincere and faithful spirit.

For these causes, declaring thee fallen again into your old errors, and under the sentence of excommunication which you have formerly incurred, WE DECREE THAT YOU ART A RELAPSED HERETIC, by our present sentence which, seated in tribunal, we utter and pronounce in this writing; we denounce thee as a rotten member, and that you may not vitiate others, as cast out from the unity of the Church, separate from her Body, abandoned to the secular power as, indeed, by these presents, we do cast thee off, separate and abandon thee; - praying this same secular power, so far as concerns death and the mutilation of the limbs, to moderate its judgment towards thee, and, if true signs of penitence should appear in thee, [to permit] that the Sacrament of Penance be administered to thee.

We, the Judges, say and decree that you have been on the subject of thy pretended divine revelations and apparitions lying, seducing, pernicious, presumptuous, lightly believing, rash, superstitious, a divineress and blasphemer towards God and the Saints, a despiser of God Himself in His Sacraments; a prevaricator of the Divine Law, of sacred doctrine and of ecclesiastical sanctions; seditious, cruel, apostate, schismatic, erring on many points of our Faith, and by all these means rashly guilty towards God and Holy Church.

And also, because that often, very often, not only by Us on Our part but by Doctors and Masters learned and expert, full of zeal for the salvation of thy soul, you have been duly and sufficiently warned to amend, to correct thyself and to submit to the disposal, decision, and correction of Holy Mother Church, which you have not willed, and have always obstinately refused to do, having even expressly and many times refused to submit thyself to our Lord the Pope and to the General Council; for these causes, as hardened and obstinate in thy crimes, excesses and errors, WE DECLARE THEE OF RIGHT EXCOMMUNICATE AND HERETIC; and after your errors have been destroyed in a public preaching,

We declare that you must be abandoned and that We do abandon thee to the secular authority, as a member of Satan, separate from the Church, infected with the leprosy of heresy, in order that you may not corrupt also the other members of Christ; praying this same power, that, as concerns death and the mutilation of

Joan of Arc, that brave maiden heroine and liberator of Orléans, was cruelly sentenced to death by burning. It was a standard inquisitorial method of execution, and one of the cruelest known to man. Death by burning is the most awful way to go. The English hated her so fervently, that they would not (and could not) grant her a more swifter and merciful death.

Before the execution, Joan was placed in a cart and taken through Rouen's streets. She was forced to wear a cap with the words "relapsed heretic, apostate, idolater." A crude scaffold was erected at the marketplace. Many gathered to view her last moments on this earth, and the scene of her execution was thus saved for posterity by many eyewitness accounts. They said Joan was calm and composed as the sentence and the sermon were read to her. When it was her time to address the crowd, she reportedly broke down weeping and said that she forgave her accusers and executioners for what they were doing and were about to do and asked that they pray for her. It is noted in most of these accounts that by the end of Joan's emotional address to the crowd, many of the judges and the assessors, several English soldiers and officials, and many people from the crowd - were openly sobbing. Ultimately, however, the time for Joan to die came, and the executioner was ordered to "do his duty."

Joan was tied to a tall pillar, around which brush was gathered. The pillar was raised above the level of the crowd, so all could witness her demise. Before the sentence was carried out, Joan asked for a cross, to look at it while she died. A sympathetic English soldier quickly made one out of sticks of wood, and held it up before her. The next moment, a proper crucifix was brought from the nearby church, and one Friar Martin Ladvenu held it high up in front of Joan, allowing her to look at it as the flames swelled around her.

Several eyewitnesses recalled that she repeatedly screamed *"...in a loud voice the holy name of Jesus, and implored and invoked, without ceasing, the aid of the saints of Paradise"*. Then her head drooped, and it was over.

After the execution, her remains were gathered and thrown unceremoniously into the Seine river.

Many were moved beyond measure by the death of the famed Joan of Arc. The Secretary to the King of England, Jean Tressard, was seen returning from the execution in great sadness and anger, claiming *"We are all ruined, for a good and holy person was burned."* Even the Cardinal of England and the Bishop of Therouanne were said to have wept bitterly after the event. The executioner, later revealed to have been one Geoffroy Therage, confessed to Friar Martin Ladvenu and admitted that *"he had a great fear of being damned, as he had burned a saint."* The English began panicking, thinking a public "cult following" would form. They began punishing all those speaking publicly in her favor—many surviving documents related to the prosecution a few days after Joan's execution.

It was not until November of 1449, near the end of the war, when the English were ultimately expelled from Rouen, that the gradual process of appealing Joan's case was set in motion. This process eventually led to a posthumous acquittal pronounced by Inquisitor Jean Brehal, who, ironically, had been associated with an institution under English influence during the war. Brehal concluded that she had been unlawfully and unjustly convicted by a corrupt court driven by *"...evident malice against the Roman Catholic Church and, indeed, heresy."* The Inquisitor and other theologians consulted for the appeal and thus condemned Cauchon and the other judges while hailing Joan as a martyr. His lengthy speech included the following brief excerpt:

"...And carefully considering each and all of the other points which must be considered and scrutinized in this matter; seated in judgment and with eyes fixed only upon God, by this our definitive verdict which we hand down in this rescript while seated in judgment: We state and pronounce, decree and declare the aforesaid trial and sentence - being filled with fraud,

false charges, injustice, contradiction, and manifest errors concerning both fact and law - together with the aforementioned abjuration, execution and all that resulted, to have been, to be, and will be null, without effect, void, and of no consequence.

And notwithstanding, [i.e., despite the obvious invalidity] if there is any need to do so, we, as reason demands, hereby nullify, void, and annul them [the results of the original trial] and entirely strip them of all effect, declaring that the aforesaid Joan and her family the plaintiffs did not contract or incur any mark or stain of disrepute as a result of the above mentioned matter; and [also declaring] that she is and will be freed and cleansed from the aforementioned; and if such should be necessary, also completely exonerating her."

These developments laid the groundwork for her eventual beatification in 1909 and canonization as a saint in 1920. By that time, even English writers and clergy no longer harbored the opposition that their predecessors had displayed. During World War I, amidst the ongoing canonization process and a period of French-English reconciliation, Allied soldiers paid homage to this courageous figure by invoking her name on battlefields not far from where she herself had fought.

Chapter VII: A Vision in the Flames

The Armagnacs lost their symbol and their famed heroine, Joan of Arc. With her death, the war was not changed. Her triumphs during her brief military career were instrumental in raising Armagnac morale. As a result, the English could not regain the momentum they had previously. Charles VII remained the King of France. In 1431, his English rival, the 10-year-old Henry VI, was crowned in Paris as a rival King, but without any serious consequence. Four years later, in 1435, the Burgundians abandoned their alliance with the English after signing the Treaty of Arras. Ultimately, 22 years after Joan of Arc was executed, the Hundred Years' War ended in 1453 after the Battle of Castillon. The war ended as a French victory, and the English were finally expelled from France.

But was Joan's death in vain? Not if we consider her significant victories. Still, her death did bear weight for King Charles VII. While the war was still on, Joan's execution placed him in a precarious position and created a political liability for him. This is because it was automatically implied - to his enemies and allies - that his coronation as the King was achieved through the actions of an executed heretic. Because of this, in 1450, Charles VII ordered an inquest to be opened regarding Joan's trial and execution. For this task, he employed a noted theologian and the former rector of the University of Paris, Guillaume Bouille. The man's brief investigation quickly concluded that the judgment of Joan as a heretic was arbitrary. In this process, he interviewed seven witnesses. It was agreed that Joan of Arc was a prisoner of war but still treated as a political prisoner. It was also decided that she was killed without basis. Still, this report could not overturn the verdict. It was an important stepping stone toward a later retrial.

One year before the war ended in 1452, Cardinal Guillaume d'Estouteville, the papal legate and King Charles's relative, along with Jean Brehal, opened a second inquest into Joan's trial and execution. He interviewed 20 witnesses and presented 27 articles about the thoroughly biased trial. For the next two years, d'Estouteville worked diligently on this case. In 1454, Bréhal acted as the intermediary for a petition addressed to Pope Nicholas V from Joan's mother, Isabelle, and her two brothers, Jean and Pierre. Bréhal forwarded this petition to the Pope. Bréhal subsequently summarized his findings to theologians, legal experts in France, Italy, and even a professor at the University of Vienna.The majority of these individuals expressed favorable opinions regarding Joan. Following the death of Pope Nicholas V in early 1455, his successor, Pope Callixtus III, granted permission for a trial of rehabilitation and appointed three commissioners to oversee the proceedings: Jean Juvénal des Ursins, the Archbishop of Reims; Guillaume Chartier, the Bishop of Paris; and Richard Olivier de Longueil, the Bishop of Coutances. Among these commissioners, Bréhal was chosen to serve as the Inquisitor. The rehabilitation trial commenced on November 7, 1455, at Notre Dame Cathedral, where Joan's mother publicly presented a formal plea for her daughter's rehabilitation. The proceedings concluded on July 7, 1456, at Rouen Cathedral after testimonies were heard from approximately 115 witnesses.

The court found that the original trial was biased, deceitful, and unjust - through and through. The abjuration which Joan signed, her execution and their consequences were nullified. It was furthermore summarized that Pierre Cuachon, the original inquisitor, could be guilty of malice and heresy. To drive these decisions home, the Articles of Accusation that were initially presented at the execution of Joan were ceremoniously torn up almost two decades later. Furthermore, the court ordered that an elaborate stone cross be erected on the site of Joan's martyr-like execution.

At this point, we must reflect on some of the more enigmatic aspects of Joan of Arc's story. Perhaps the most mysterious was her visions. Today, in the 21st century, we might look upon such terms with skepticism, but in the Middle Ages, such things were viewed with awe and disbelief. Could it be that Joan indeed saw saints and angels? As we know, Joan claimed to have experienced visions and divine revelations throughout her life and until her dying moment. These visions played a significant role in shaping her beliefs, actions, and ultimate mission. Joan's own accounts during her trial stated that she began receiving visions from a young age, around the age of 13. These visions were primarily auditory and visual in nature, involving the appearance of heavenly figures and voices.

It was during these visions that Joan claimed to have received specific instructions regarding military tactics, the raising of a military force, and the eventual lifting of the siege of Orléans, a critical turning point in the Hundred Years' War. Joan's visions also guided her in matters of strategy and decision-making throughout her military campaigns.

These supernatural experiences shaped Joan's sense of purpose and inspired her with unwavering faith and determination. Her steadfast conviction in the authenticity and significance of her visions played a crucial role in rallying support and boosting morale among the French troops.

Visions, as experienced by individuals like Joan of Arc and others, are subjective phenomena that fall within the realm of human perception and cognition. From a scientific perspective, visions are often attributed to a combination of neurological and psychological factors. Neurologically, visions can be linked to various brain processes and functions. For example, certain medical conditions or alterations in brain activity, such as epilepsy, migraines, or hallucinogenic substances, can induce visual hallucinations or altered states of consciousness that may resemble visions. These experiences can be attributed to abnormal electrical activity, neurotransmitter imbalances, or changes in sensory processing within the brain. Psychologically, visions can be influenced by a person's beliefs, emotions, and expectations.

Factors such as religious or cultural upbringing, personal experiences, and suggestibility can shape the content and interpretation of visions.

Additionally, the human brain has a remarkable capacity for generating mental imagery, and visions can be seen as a product of this imaginative process. It is important to note that scientific understanding of visions is still limited, and not all aspects of these experiences can be fully explained or understood at present. The subjective nature of visions makes it challenging to study them in a controlled scientific manner. Furthermore, individual interpretations and cultural contexts play a significant role in shaping the meaning and significance attributed to visions.

In summary, the science behind visions involves exploring the neurological and psychological mechanisms that underlie these experiences. While some aspects can be explained through brain processes and psychological factors, visions remain complex and multifaceted phenomena that continue to be a subject of scientific inquiry and exploration. However, today, we cannot possibly know what influenced Joan's visions - and if they even existed at all.

Another topic that is often scrutinized and

questioned is Joan of Arc's cross-dressing. She is known to have worn men's clothes and armor throughout her military career. At the time, however, it was a radical move for a young woman to wear male apparel. During the trial, her choice of clothing was classified as heresy and was the topic of five of the 12 articles of accusation. Joan also wore her hair closely cropped, just like men wore it. When questioned, however, Joan could not explain why she decided to dress outside the norm for women. To her, it was simply a choice and likely a necessity in times of war. She said she did it by the command of God and his angels. She claimed she would return to wearing female clothes once her calling was fulfilled. Was her choice of apparel a just reason for her vicious death? While such practices were considered sinful, the church's position on the matter was unclear. Thomas Aquinas stated that a woman might wear a man's clothes to hide from enemies or if no other clothes were available.

As we know, Joan did both, wearing them in enemy territory to get to Chinon and in her prison cell after her abjuration when her dress was taken from her. So, did she genuinely commit a sin? Or was it the most convenient thing for her enemies to put against her? Furthermore, Joan of Arc might have chosen men's clothes to deter potential rapists or persistent suitors and thus remain a virgin - a primary aspect of her divine mission. Due to all this, Joan of Arc is often regarded as a figure who transcended traditional gender roles during her time. In a society where women's roles were confined mainly to domestic spheres, Joan defied societal norms and expectations by actively participating in military and political affairs. Her unwavering determination, leadership, and courage challenged prevailing notions of gender limitations. Joan claimed her divine mission to lead the French army and actively took command, strategized military campaigns, and inspired soldiers on the battlefield. She wore men's clothing, which was unconventional for a woman of her time, and asserted her authority in male-dominated spaces.

Despite being a young peasant woman, Joan's ability to gain the respect and loyalty of soldiers

and commanders speaks to her exceptional
qualities and the profound impact she had on
those around her. Her actions and successes
challenged the prevailing gender hierarchy,
highlighting that women could possess qualities
traditionally associated with male leadership. It is
important to note that Joan's actions were met
with both admiration and skepticism during her
lifetime. While many revered her as a symbol of
courage and divine inspiration, others questioned
her motivations and legitimacy. Her trial and
subsequent martyrdom were partly influenced by
societal discomfort with a woman transgressing
established gender roles and engaging in
traditionally male domains. Even so, Joan of Arc's
remarkable story inspires and resonates with
people, particularly those seeking to challenge
gender norms and advocate for gender equality.
Her legacy is a reminder that individuals can
transcend societal expectations and make a
lasting impact, regardless of gender.

Some five centuries after her death, Joan of Arc
was officially sainted. Saint Joan of Arc is a saint
of the Roman Catholic Church. She was beatified

by Pope Pius X in 1909 and canonized on 16 May 1920 by Pope Benedict XV. Her feast day is 30 May, the anniversary of her execution. Besides this, Joan left behind her a significant legacy. It is profound and far-reaching, transcending the boundaries of time and geography. Her impact can be seen in various realms, including history, culture, religion, and gender equality. For example, she is considered a national symbol of France. Her pivotal role in the Hundred Years' War and her unwavering dedication to the French cause have cemented her position as an emblem of French patriotism. She is celebrated for her contribution to the country's history and her ability to inspire unity and resilience.

Her legacy is also religious. Joan's claims of divine guidance and her deep faith have made her an enduring inspiration within Christianity. Her steadfast devotion and belief in fulfilling God's will have resonated with believers throughout the ages. Joan's story inspires religious devotion, spiritual contemplation, and theological discussions. Uniquely, her legacy inspires the feminist movements of today. Joan of

Arc's defiance of gender roles and her extraordinary achievements in a male-dominated world has made her an iconic figure for feminists and advocates of gender equality. Her ability to command armies, lead troops into battle, and challenge societal norms has made her a symbol of empowerment for women and a testament to their potential in traditionally male spheres.

Needless to say, Joan's story has captivated the imaginations of writers, playwrights, poets, and artists across the centuries. Numerous works of literature, theater, music, and visual arts have been inspired by her life and exploits. From Shakespeare's play "Henry VI" to Mark Twain's historical novel "Personal Recollections of Joan of Arc," her story continues to be a source of creative inspiration. Such an incredible life story cannot fail but inspire people from all walks of life. Ultimately, Joan of Arc's impact on history and culture cannot be overstated. Her trial and martyrdom have raised questions about justice, religious persecution, and political manipulation. Her story has been dissected and analyzed from various perspectives, contributing to historical scholarship and the understanding of medieval Europe. Overall, Joan of Arc's legacy encompasses bravery, faith, resilience, and the ability to challenge the status quo. She serves as a reminder that individuals, regardless of their background or gender, can make a profound impact on the world by standing up for their beliefs and fighting for what they deem right.

Conclusion

Ultimately, Joan's story is a story of selfless sacrifice. Willingly, she cast aside her life, her prospects, and her future. Instead, she committed onto a path that was nothing but sacrifice, and she cared not. Her sacrifice was multi-dimensional. On the battlefield, Joan fearlessly led the French army, inspiring troops and rallying them to victory. Her presence on the frontlines, where danger and death were ever-present, showed her unwavering commitment to liberating her country from foreign occupation.

Joan's selflessness extended beyond the battlefield. Throughout her trial, she endured harsh interrogations, manipulation, and ultimately faced accusations of heresy. Yet, she never wavered in her steadfast belief and refused to compromise her convictions. Her sacrifice was rooted in staying true to her divine mission, even in the face of immense personal adversity. We can only stand awe-inspired and admire such perseverance. Joan's selflessness was not motivated by personal ambition or gain. It was fueled by a deep love for her country and her people, coupled with an unwavering belief in her divine mission. Her sacrifice definitely reminds us of the power of selflessness.

In the end, Joan's sacrifice reached its climax when she willingly accepted her fate on the execution pyre. Rather than renouncing her beliefs to save her life, she chose to embrace martyrdom. Her sacrifice became a beacon of inspiration for future generations, a testament to the lengths one can go to uphold principles and defend what is just. How strong her belief was - how inspiring and poignant her faith! We can only ask ourselves the question - could our resolve, bravery, devotion, and selflessness match Joan's? Could you stare at the flaming execution pyre and stay calm and true to your life's calling? This is a puzzling question to ponder.

In this exploration of Joan's life, we have witnessed her extraordinary journey, one that transcended gender roles and shattered societal expectations. From the whispers of divine guidance to the battlefields where her indomitable spirit blazed, she forged her path with unwavering determination and unwavering belief in her mission. Joan of Arc's legacy is not simply that of a fearless warrior or a visionary leader; it is a testament to the power of resilience, faith, and the human spirit. She showed us that the strength to defy conventions lies within us all, waiting to be awakened by our unwavering conviction and audacious dreams. Through her words and actions, Joan beckons us to embrace our own inner strength, to rise above the limitations imposed by society, and to strive for what we believe is right. She reminds us that courage knows no gender, that determination has no boundaries, and that the pursuit of justice is a noble cause worthy of sacrifice.

As we close the pages of this book, let us carry Joan's legacy in our hearts, empowering us to confront our battles and conquer our doubts. Let her story ignite a fire within us, propelling us forward in the face of adversity and reminding us that we can leave an indelible mark on the world. May the spirit of Joan of Arc forever inspire us to be unyielding in our pursuit of truth, to stand tall in the face of opposition, and to champion the causes that ignite our passion. In embracing her courage, we unlock our boundless potential and become the heroes of our own stories.

References:

Halsall, P. 1996. *Medieval Sourcebook: Joan of Arc: Letter to the King of England, 1429.* Fordham University.

Hobbins, D. 2005. *The Trial of Joan of Arc.* Harvard University Press.

Linder, O. D. 2023. *The Trial of Joan of Arc: An Account.* Famous Trials.

Rea, C. *The Maiden of France: A Brief Overview of Joan of Arc and the Siege of Orléans.* Cam Rea.

Ringbom, J. 2010. *French Nationalism and Joan of Arc.*

Vale, G. A. M. and Lanhers, Y. 2018. *Joan of Arc. Warrior, Military Leader (c. 1412–1431).* Britannica.

Williamson, A. *The Posthumous Declaration of Innocence.* Joan of Arc Archive.

www.ingramcontent.com/pod-product-compliance
Lightning Source LLC
Chambersburg PA
CBHW021011160726
47994CB00006B/2468